To my partners in snowstorm fun:

Mila, Leila, and Nesha

Our experience during such a strange time filled us with immense gratitude for things we typically take for granted. While it was not easy, we knew that our hardship was only temporary. We have never had to worry about having enough food to eat or having access to clean water. Since we know we are very lucky and others do not have this luxury, a portion of proceeds from this book will go towards:

Central Texas Food Bank

The Central Texas Food Bank is the largest hunger-relief charity in Central Texas and has fought against hunger since 1981. They share free food and knowledge on low-cost, healthy eating with families in need; assist families who qualify for federal assistance programs; and make food affordable for charitable and government partners. They work with roughly 300 Partner Agencies across 21 counties in Texas to end hunger; their work spans an area of nearly 20,000 miles. The Central Texas Food Bank receives a top four-star rating from Charity Navigator, spending over 96% of the funds it receives on the programs and services it offers with 100% accountability/transparency.

Water Mission

Water Mission builds safe water, sanitation, and hygiene solutions in developing nations and disaster areas. With their comprehensive approach, they design customized solutions for each community they serve and partner with the recipients throughout the process. They have received a top four-star rating on Charity Navigator for thirteen straight years, with 100% accountability/transparency and 88% of funds going directly to programs. To date, they have served over 7 million people across 2,800 projects in 51 countries.
With their 100% promise, 100% of donations will go towards building water wells.

FIRST EDITION

Snow in our Potties!

The Storm Made Us Do It

Written By Maya Noronha Duff ❄ Illustrated By Christina Commons

For Texans, snow has always had a certain mystique,
But one year, we had a most unexpected week!

After sleeping through a very cold night,
We woke to the city in a blanket of white.

Nearly the whole state of Texas was all shut down;
The snow made it too hard to get around.

Though we couldn't get food, our pantries were loaded.
(For this was still during the pandemic of COVID).

With coats and jammies (since we had no snow pants),

We delighted in this unusual chance

To make snow angels on the very same lawn
That's green and grassy the whole year long.

We made snow ice cream!

And baked fresh bread.

Then cruised down hills in our "Texas sled"!

Our littlest sister tried to eat all the snow-
(hopefully the white, and not the yellow)!

To make our own candy like pioneer lasses,

On a pan full of snow, we poured hot molasses.

Hot cocoa and marshmallows were such a treat
That warmed us right up from our heads to our feet.

Some of our friends had no power for days.
They were so cold, by the fire they stayed.

Folks burned furniture to make firewood;

We would have had them all over, if we could!

One friend lost water and power in one swoop;
(They searched for snow to melt with no deer poop!)

Others lit lanterns and played games of cards,
They made it fun, but being cold was so hard!

Families snuggled together throughout the storm;
Their body heat helped to keep them warm.

On Day Number 3 of all the snow fun,
Our running water decided it was all done.

We had bathtubs and pots
filled with water and snow;

(We used it for flushing when we had to "go").

It felt like we were living in frontier days,
'Til the Mars Rover landed and had us amazed.

Our family was lucky we never lost power
(and some of us were glad to be skipping a shower!)

No water for FIVE days and Mom thought:

"Let's bathe the kids in a crawfish pot!"

CONTACT!

The very next day, the sun started to glow.
We filled buckets and tubs with melting snow.

Once taken for granted, now we really knew
That water is most precious for me and for you.

Despite the unusual and
treacherous weather,

Texans showed strength
as we banded together.

When electricity failed many
because of the ice,

Neighbors made stations
to charge a device.

Strangers rescued each other
from cars that were stranded;

A man jumped in a pool
where his doggy had landed.

Sea turtles were struggling just to survive,
People moved them inside so that they could thrive.

Strangers and neighbors gave water and food
It really was quite a cooperative mood.

The storms have now passed; normal life has returned.
But we'll never forget our experience or
the lessons we learned.

Electricity, clean water, enough food to eat-
What was our norm now feels quite elite.

Many people's basic needs go unmet,
Which can make us all feel very upset!

But though we are children,
there are things we can do.
We can make the world great
for me and for you!

About the Author

Maya Noronha Duff lives in Austin, Texas with her husband and three children. She had an irrational amount of fun during the Texas snowstorms of 2021. (And afterwards, using every drop of harvested snow to water plants for a month!) This is her first book, but she can often be found making up rhyming songs off the top of her head to her kids Her Greatest Hits include "Two Little Poops in Here" and "Rice and Chicky Today".

About the Illustrator

Christina Commons grew up and currently resides in Oregon, which gets a little snow now and then. She has been drawing her entire life, starting with a set of markers disguised as drumsticks. She later attended the University of Oregon where she studied traditional as well as digital art mediums, earning her bachelor's degree in the latter. She has been creating professionally ever since.

www.ingramcontent.com/pod-product-compliance
Ingram Content Group UK Ltd.
Pitfield, Milton Keynes, MK11 3LW, UK
UKHW061940050826
14089UKWH00045BA/211
9780578960234